STATE V. PEYTON

Third Edition

Case File

Trial Materials

STATE V. PEYTON

Third Edition

Case File

Trial Materials

Elizabeth I. Boals
Assistant Professor of Law
Director, Center for Excellence in Advocacy
Stetson University College of Law

NATIONAL INSTITUTE FOR TRIAL ADVOCACY

Address inquiries to:
Reprint Permission
National Institute for Trial Advocacy
325 W. South Boulder RD., Ste. 1
Louisville, CO 80027-1130
Phone: (800) 225-6482
Fax: (720) 890-7069
E-mail: permissions@nita.org

ISBN 978-1-60156-952-3
FBA 1952
eISBN 978-1-60156-953-0
eFBA 1553

Printed in the United States of America

Official co-publisher of NITA.
WKLegaledu.com/NITA

CONTENTS

ACKNOWLEDGMENTS vii

INTRODUCTION 1

CASE SUMMARY 3

INSTRUCTIONS 5

REQUIRED STIPULATIONS 7

CASE MATERIALS AND EXHIBITS

Indictment of Jordan Peyton 11
    Exhibit 1—Audio Recording of Addison 911 Call 13
    Exhibit 2—Transcript of Addison 911 Call 15
    Exhibit 3—Police Report, 05-15-YR-1, Peyton Arrest 17
    Exhibit 4—BAC Results 21
    Exhibit 5—Sunset Bar & Grill Receipt (unsigned copy) 23
Statement of Jordan Peyton 25
    Exhibit 6—Photograph of Peyton & Dalton signage 29
    Exhibit 7—Peyton Driving Record 31
    Exhibit 8—Peyton Criminal Record 33
    Exhibit 9— Police Report of 05-25-YR-1 re: Evidence Collection 35
    Exhibit 10—Peyton Vehicle Registration 37
    Exhibit 11—Search Warrant and Inventory Sheet 39
    Exhibit 12—Intersection Diagram 41
    Exhibit 13—Body Camera Video 43
    Exhibit 14—Photograph of Addison Vehicle (Rear View 1) 45
    Exhibit 15—Photograph of Addison Vehicle (Rear View 2) 47
    Exhibit 16—Photograph of Addison Vehicle (Damage) 49
    Exhibit 17—Photograph of Peyton Vehicle (Damage) 51
    Exhibit 18— Photograph of Measured Scratches on Peyton Vehicle Compared to Addison Vehicle ... 53
Statement of Riley Cameron 55
    Exhibit 19—Riley Cameron Tweets 57
Preliminary Hearing Transcript: Addison 59
    Exhibit 20—Photographs of Addison Hand Injury 65
    Exhibit 21—Addison Vehicle Repair Receipt 67
Preliminary Hearing Transcript: Carter 69
    Exhibit 22—Sunset Bar & Grill Receipt (signed copy) 75
    Exhibit 23—Police Report, 08-01-YR-1, Supplemental Report 77
    Exhibit 24—Nita City Post Article re: Sunset Bar & Grill Fire 79
    Exhibit 25—Email from Defense Attorney re: Diagrams 81

Exhibit 25A—Map from Sunset Grill to Riley Cameron's Apartment (with route marked) 82

Exhibit 25B—Map from Sunset Grill to Riley Cameron's Apartment (without route marked). 83

EXPERT WITNESS TESTIMONY

State Expert Case Analysis: Williams 87

State Expert Curriculum Vitae: Williams 91

Defense Expert Case Analysis: Montgomery. 93

Defense Expert Curriculum Vitae: Montgomery 97

MEDICAL RECORDS

Exhibit 26—Affidavit to Certify Records 99

Exhibit 27—Hospital Discharge Summary Form 101

Exhibit 28—Nita Primary Physicians Group Medical Visit 103

Exhibit 29—Second Nita Primary Physicians Group Medical Visit 105

APPENDICES

Nita Statutes 109

Section 4–101 Duty of Driver to Stop, Etc., in Event of Accident Involving Injury
or Death or Damage to Attended Property 109

Section 6–101 Driving Motor Vehicle under the Influence of Intoxicants. 109

Section 6–201 Implied Consent to Post-Arrest Testing to Determine Drug or
Alcohol Content of Blood 109

Section 6–202 Presumptions from Alcohol Content of Blood 109

Section 10–101 Admissibility of Certified Court and Agency Records 110

Section 10–107 Admissibility of Blood Alcohol Content Test Results. 110

Case Law. 111

Failure to Wear a Seat Belt 111

"Intent" Element for Hit and Run 111

Admissibility of Breath Test 111

Related Materials. 113

Information on Burns. 113

Information on Breath Tests and Intoxilyzer. 115

PROPOSED JURY INSTRUCTIONS 117

JURY VERDICT FORM 119

Acknowledgments

The author would like to acknowledge The Honorable Michael D. Mason of the Circuit Court for Montgomery County, Maryland, for his insightful suggestions on this publication. The author also acknowledges the special contributions by Stetson University College of Law (SUCOL) students, Alicia Roddenberg and Meghan O'Connell, for assisting with editing and creating exhibits for this third edition of the case file and teacher's manual.

The National Institute for Trial Advocacy wishes to thank Twitter for its permission to use likenesses of its website as part of these teaching materials.

Introduction

This case file contains materials for the trial of a defendant charged with driving under the influence of intoxicants and felonious hit and run. These materials are designed to provide opportunities for this case file's users to consider criminal trial issues, including medical expert testimony, character evidence, criminal conviction impeachment, bias impeachment, prior recorded testimony, and evidence in the form of an audio-recorded 911 call, body camera footage, and a breath test computer printout.

The author hopes that this case file will familiarize attorneys with the many challenges that are an integral part of the preparation and presentation of a criminal case in modern courts of law.

CASE SUMMARY

A grand jury charged Jordan Peyton with driving under the influence of intoxicants and felony hit and run for failing to stop at the scene after she allegedly struck an occupied parked car, causing property damage and personal injury.

At the time of the incident, Peyton was thirty-six years old, five-feet, nine-inches tall, and weighed 175 pounds. She is a founding partner at the architecture firm of Peyton & Dalton, Inc., in Nita City, Nita. On May 15, YR-1, Peyton attended a social event after work. The event was held at the Sunset Bar & Grill. Peyton drove herself and a firm intern, Riley Cameron, to the event.

According to Peyton, she consumed two twelve-ounce bottles of beer at the event between 5:30 and 7:30 p.m. She claims that she did not have any other alcohol that day. Also according to Peyton, Cameron had approximately five twelve-ounce bottles of beer during the two-hour event. Peyton gave Cameron a ride home from the event.

At approximately 7:35 p.m. on May 15, YR-1, Taylor Addison, a carpenter, was sitting in her Chevy Trailblazer parked along the curb on Second Avenue facing the intersection of Second Avenue and North Market Street. She was holding a cup of extremely hot coffee. Addison took the lid off the cup to let it cool down. Addison was looking down at some papers when she sensed a car pull up on her left. Without warning, Addison's car jerked to the right. The coffee sloshed over the rim of the cup and severely burned her left hand. Addison frantically grabbed for napkins from the passenger seat to soak up the spilled coffee. She looked up and saw a silver or white Mercedes driving slowly on North Market away from the intersection. Addison honked her horn. She saw that the Mercedes had a company sign on the passenger door that said "Peyton & Dalton." As soon as she got the coffee spill under control, she called 911 from her cell phone.

Officer Lee Baldwin arrived on the scene and took Addison's statement. Using the computer in her cruiser, Officer Baldwin ran an internet search on local businesses named "Peyton & Dalton." Only one local business had that name. She cross-referenced the list of employees from the company's website with Department of Motor Vehicles records. A silver Mercedes was registered to one of the firm's partners, Jordan Peyton, at an address just a few miles from the scene. Officer Baldwin drove to Peyton's address, where she saw a silver Mercedes, with a magnetic sign that read "Peyton & Dalton" affixed to the passenger side door, in the process of parallel parking on the street in front of Peyton's house. Officer Baldwin approached the car and spoke briefly to Peyton. She determined that Peyton had been driving through the intersection of Second Avenue and North Market Street approximately thirty minutes earlier. Peyton denied hitting Addison's car. Officer Baldwin observed some scratches on the passenger side of Peyton's car that appeared to her to be consistent with the scratches on Addison's Trailblazer.

During Officer Baldwin's conversation with Peyton, she smelled a slight odor of alcohol coming from Peyton's breath and observed that her eyes were glassy and bloodshot. Peyton admitted to having two beers over a two-hour time period earlier that evening. Officer Baldwin asked Peyton to perform three field sobriety tests. In Officer Baldwin's opinion, Peyton's admission to drinking, physical appearance, and performance on the field sobriety tests indicated that she was driving under the influence of alcohol. Officer Baldwin captured the field sobriety tests with her body camera.

Officer Baldwin placed Peyton under arrest for driving under the influence of intoxicants and felony hit and run. During a search incident to formal arrest, Officer Baldwin found a credit card receipt in Peyton's blazer pocket from the Sunset Bar & Grill, dated that same evening. Peyton was very upset and demanded that her blood alcohol content level (BAC) be tested. Officer Baldwin transported her to the police station and brought her into the DUI processing center. At 9:30 p.m., Officer Baldwin administered the BAC exam on an Intoxilyzer. The reading was 0.06. In Nita, BAC must be 0.08 or more for the prosecution to obtain a presumption that the individual was driving under the influence of alcohol.

The applicable law is contained in the statutes and proposed jury instructions set forth at the end of this case file.

All years in these materials are stated in the following form:

1) YR-0 indicates the actual year in which the case is being tried (i.e., the present year);

2) YR-1 indicates the next preceding year (please use the actual year);

3) YR-2 indicates the second preceding year (please use the actual year), etc.

Color copies of the exhibits, the audio of the 911 telephone call, and the body camera video are available online at:

http://bit.ly/1P20Jea

Password: Peyton3

INSTRUCTIONS

Unless otherwise instructed, a party need not call all of the witnesses on their list. All witnesses are gender neutral and can be played by either a man or a woman. Witnesses may not deny that they made a prior statement that is contained in their signed statement or prior testimony. Jordan Peyton may be called only in her own defense.

Version I

State:	Officer Lee Baldwin
	Taylor Addison
Defense:	Jordan Peyton
	Riley Cameron

Version II

State:	Officer Lee Baldwin
	Taylor Addison
	Doctor Kipper Williams
Defense:	Jordan Peyton
	Riley Cameron
	Doctor Fran Montgomery

REQUIRED STIPULATIONS

1) The parties agree that the Intoxilyzer machine used to test Jordan Peyton's blood alcohol content on May 15, YR-1, was properly calibrated and in good working condition.

2) The parties agree that, according to the laboratory tests, the paint samples taken from Taylor Addison's car and Jordan Peyton's car contained only paint consistent with the car from which the scrapings were collected. There was no evidence of paint transfers on either car.

3) The parties agree that the certified criminal record and driving record for Jordan Peyton, and the criminal record for Taylor Addison are accurate and authentic. These certified copies, if relevant and otherwise admissible, shall be admitted without the testimony of the custodian of these records pursuant to Nita Criminal Code § 10-101.

4) The parties agree that the 911 emergency call recording, provided as Exhibit 1, is an accurate and complete recording of the entire 911 call placed by Taylor Addison on May 15, YR-1, at 7:38 p.m. The parties further stipulate that the transcript of this 911 call, provided in Exhibit 2, is an accurate and complete transcription.

5) The defense made motions to suppress, on Fourth and Fifth Amendment grounds: (1) the Sunset Bar & Grill receipt found in Jordan Peyton's blazer pocket when she was searched pursuant to her arrest; (2) Jordan Peyton's oral statements to Officer Baldwin during her stop and arrest; and (3) the May 16, YR-1 written statement made by Jordan Peyton. On these grounds, the court denied the motions.

6) The parties stipulate that both the body camera video and audio are authentic and accurately represent the portion of the stop of Jordan Peyton that they appear to portray. The parties further stipulate that the video and audio cut off due to a mechanical error near the end of the encounter between Officer Baldwin and Jordan Peyton. The mechanical error was not the fault of Office Baldwin.

Case Materials and Exhibits

IN THE CIRCUIT COURT FOR THE CITY OF NITA

THE PEOPLE OF   )
    THE STATE OF NITA   )
)

    v.   )   Case No. CR 1112
)

JORDAN PEYTON   )
)

    Defendant.   )

INDICTMENT

The Grand Jury in and for the City of Nita, State of Nita, upon its oath and in the name and by the authority of the State of Nita, does hereby charge the following offenses under the Criminal Code of the State of Nita:

COUNT I

That on May 15, YR-1, within the City of Nita in the State of Nita, JORDAN PEYTON committed the crime of

FELONIOUS HIT AND RUN

in violation of Section 4-101 of the Nita Criminal Code of YR-27 as amended, in that JORDAN PEYTON was the driver of a motor vehicle involved in an accident in which a person was injured or an occupied vehicle was damaged and did not immediately stop as close to the scene of the accident as possible and report personal information as required under Section 4-101.

COUNT II

That on May 15, YR-1, within the City of Nita in the State of Nita, JORDAN PEYTON committed the crime of

DRIVING UNDER THE INFLUENCE OF INTOXICANTS

in violation of Section 6-101 of the Nita Criminal Code of YR-27, as amended, in that JORDAN PEYTON drove or operated a motor vehicle while under the influence of alcohol, which impaired JORDAN PEYTON'S ability to drive or operate a motor vehicle safely.

Exhibit 1

Audio Recording of Addison 911 Call

Audio of the 911 telephone call is available online at:

http://bit.ly/1P20Jea
Password: Peyton3

Exhibit 2

Transcript of Addison 911 Call

Date: May 15, YR-1

Time: 7:38 p.m.

Caller: Taylor Addison

Police Department Dispatcher (PDD): 911, what's your emergency?

Caller: AHHHH! Some car just hit my car and took off! My hand is really hurt!

PDD: Slow down. Slow down. What is your name?

Caller: Taylor Addison.

PDD: What happened?

Caller: OK, OK, I was in my car holding a cup of coffee, and this car sideswiped me! I can't stop the burning on my hand!

PDD: Can you give me any details about this car or the driver?

Caller: I think it was the Mercedes that hit me. I saw it head down North Market Street. Silver or white with a sign that says "Peyton & Dalton." It must be that architecture firm. I couldn't see the driver. I can't believe this! I just can't believe this.

PDD: OK, do you need any medical assistance?

Caller: Yes.

PDD: I will send a cruiser and ambulance out to you immediately. Where exactly are you?

Caller: I'm at the corner of Second Avenue and, um, North Market Street downtown Nita City. Please hurry up! My hand! Oh, my hand!

PDD: Please stay on the line until emergency assistance arrives.

Caller: Somebody had to see it. Maybe somebody saw the car that hit me. Light colored. Ah, definitely not a truck. A sedan.

Caller: I can hear the sirens. Thanks. Thank you so much.

END OF CALL

[Audio of the 911 telephone call is available online at: http://bit.ly/1P20Jea, Password: Peyton3]

Exhibit 3

PAGE 1 OF 2

STATE OF NITA

POLICE REPORT

DATE OF INCIDENT OCCURRENCE	TIME	NCIC NUMBER	OFFICER ID NUMBER	CASE NUMBER
05-15-YR-1	**7:35 p.m.**	**46768**	**679**	**CR-1112**

"X" ONE	"X" ONE	TYPE SUPPLEMENTAL ("X" APPLICABLE)		
[X] NARRATIVE	[X] CRIMINAL REPORT	[ ] COLLISION UPDATE	[ ] FATAL	[X] HIT AND RUN
[ ] SUPPLEMENTAL	[ ] OTHER	[ ] SCHOOL BUS	[ ] OTHER	

SUBJECT	REPORTING DISTRICT/BEAT	CITATION NUMBER
Arrest of Jordan Peyton	**2nd Dist.**	**N/A**

NARRATIVE:

I received a dispatch at 7:38 p.m. reporting a hit and run at the corner of Second Avenue and North Market Street in Nita City. Upon arriving at the scene, I found Taylor Addison sitting on the ground outside of her Trailblazer, which was parallel parked on Second Avenue. I observed her hand was bright red and blistering. While waiting for the ambulance, I took Addison's statement. She told me that she was sitting in her car waiting to meet with a client in a nearby business about a potential job (Addison is a carpenter). She sensed a light-colored car pull up next to her, but she didn't actually look at it because she was reviewing a document. She felt her car jerk to the right. The movement of her car caused her to spill the coffee she was holding. Hot coffee spilled all over her left hand. After spilling the coffee, she tossed the coffee cup out the window and tried to get the coffee off her hand with napkins from the passenger seat. She looked up just in time to see a silver or white Mercedes heading slowly down North Market Street away from the intersection. She saw a sign for the "Peyton & Dalton" architecture firm on the passenger door of the Mercedes. She has worked on projects with this firm so she was familiar with the name. Using the computer in my cruiser, I searched for information on the employees of the Peyton & Dalton architecture firm. The firm's internet site had a list of employees, which I cross-checked with the Department of Motor Vehicles records. A silver Mercedes was registered to one of the firm's partners, Jordan Peyton, at an address a few miles from the scene. There were no other Mercedes registered to Peyton & Dalton employees.

State of Nita	
POLICE REPORT	PAGE 2 OF 2

I observed damage to the front driver's side bumper of Addison's Trailblazer. The bumper was not dented, but the paint was scratched. Addison claims there was no previous damage to her bumper.

About this time, the ambulance arrived and the paramedics administered care to Addison. I determined that it was too dark to take quality photographs of the damage. I planned to return to the scene in the morning to collect evidence and take photographs. I proceeded to Jordan Peyton's house.

When I arrived at Peyton's residence, I parallel parked my cruiser at the curb. As I was getting out of my cruiser, I saw a silver Mercedes parallel parking a few cars ahead of me. The driver parked without incident. When the driver got out of the car, I identified myself and asked her name. She informed me that her name was Jordan Peyton. I asked if she had been the only person driving her car that day; she told me that she had been. I asked her if she had been driving her car through the intersection of Second Avenue and North Market about thirty minutes prior. She said "I think so. I was definitely on North Market. I came up First or Second Avenue to North Market." I shined my flashlight on her car and noticed light-colored scratches on the rear passenger side door panel and wheel well. I asked her about these scratches, and she said the scratches were from an accident in the parking garage at her office. These scratches appeared to me to be consistent with the damage to Addison's vehicle.

Over the course of my conversation with Peyton, I noticed a slight, yet distinct odor of alcohol on her breath. I also noticed that her eyes were glassy and bloodshot. In my experience, both of these observations indicate an individual has consumed alcohol recently. I asked her if she had been drinking that night, and she told me that she "drank two beers earlier that evening." Upon being informed of this, I activated my body camera and asked her to perform three field sobriety tests. She agreed.

1. I asked Peyton to stand on one foot with her other foot lifted approximately six inches off the ground in front of her, close her eyes, and slowly count to thirty. She asked to remove her shoes because they were slippery and muttered something under her breath about her legs hurting. At her request, I permitted her to remove her shoes. Nevertheless, she was only able to count to six when she had to put her lifted leg down to steady herself. She lifted it again and dropped it again at thirteen. She lifted it again while laughing, and using her arms for balance, was able to hold it from twenty-four to thirty, but I already considered her performance on this task a failure and consistent with being under the influence.

2. I asked her to close her eyes, tilt her head back, and put her arms straight out to the sides. Then, I asked her to slowly touch the tip of her index finger to her nose with each hand. She was able to complete this with her right hand on the first attempt. With her left hand, she unsuccessfully attempted to complete this task three times (she overshot her nose each time), but was ultimately able to complete the task on her fourth attempt. Her phone rang and she attempted to answer it during the testing. She was unsteady on her feet the

whole test, although she was able to keep her feet together during the test. I considered her performance on this task a failure and consistent with being under the influence.

3. I asked her to walk heel-to-toe in a straight line for ten steps, turn around, and then walk back heel-to-toe to her original spot. While she was able to walk ten steps forward without deviating from the imaginary line, she had to walk very slowly and use her arms for balance. She could not turn without steadying herself with one foot slightly off to the side. She also stepped off the imaginary line slightly two times on her return trip. This test took much longer than it needed to, she begged to try again because she knew she had performed badly. I denied her request. I considered her performance on this task a failure and consistent with being under the influence.

It should be noted that during the administration of the field sobriety tests Peyton did not seem to take me or the tests seriously. She was condescending and even wanted to use her cellphone during the administration of the tests. She laughed and told me this whole process was "hilarious."

Based on my ten years as a police officer making DUI arrests and all of the information I had to this point, I placed Peyton under arrest for DUI and felony hit and run and read her the complete Miranda warnings from the police department issued card. During a search incident to her arrest, I found a receipt from the Sunset Bar & Grill from earlier that same evening in her right blazer pocket. I did not ask Peyton any questions about the receipt, but she blurted out, "That's my receipt from the happy hour, but I did not drink all of those drinks." I attached the receipt to this report.

At this point, Peyton became very upset and demanded to have her blood alcohol content (BAC) tested. I was more than happy to comply with her request. Given that I did not have a breathalyzer test in my car, I drove her directly to the DUI processing center at the police station. At 9:32 p.m., Peyton gave a 210 liters breath sample to the Intoxilyzer. She had a reading of 0.06. A copy of the reading was provided to Peyton and is attached to this report.

PREPARERS NAME, RANK, AND DIVISION	DATE
BALDWIN, LEE, OFFICER, SECOND DISTRICT PATROL	**05-15-YR-1**

Exhibit 4

BAC Results

Intoxilyzer—Alcohol Analyzer

Model: 5468-DGI I

Date: May 15, YR-1

Subject Name: Peyton, Jordan

Subject DOB: 10/01/YR-36

Driver Lic. #: 356-88-463OD

Arresting Officer: Baldwin, Lee

Badge #: 679

Testing by: Baldwin, Lee

Testing Time: 9:32 p.m.

Subject Test   0.06 Alcohol Content

Exhibit 5

Sunset Bar & Grill Receipt (unsigned copy)

Sunset Bar & Grill

Your Neighborhood Bar

****

Server: Pat Carter
Date: May 15, YR-1
Time: 7:18 p.m.

. . . .

ORDER:

7 Imported Bottle Beer
@ 5.00 . . . . $35.00

Subtotal $35.00

Tax (10%) . . $03.50

Total $38.50

****

Card: xxxx xxxx xxxx 2398

Tip _____

Total _____

_____

****

THANK YOU!
PLEASE COME AGAIN

STATEMENT OF JORDAN PEYTON

1 My name is Jordan Peyton, and I am thirty-six years old, five-feet, nine-inches tall, and weigh
2 approximately 175 pounds. I reside at 1313 Randolph Road in Nita City. I am not married, and
3 I have no children. I make this written statement freely and voluntarily and without reserva-
4 tion. I waive my rights to remain silent and have an attorney present during questioning. I
5 have been in jail all night, and before I am released I want to tell my side of the story. I am a
6 founding partner at the cutting-edge architecture firm of Peyton & Dalton. I started this firm
7 with a few of my classmates after graduating first in my class from Nita College with a bach-
8 elor's degree in architectural design in YR-11. Peyton & Dalton has five partners and fifteen
9 associates. We also employ college interns—usually around ten interns at any given time.
10
11 I am best known for my work on commercial building designs. My designs have been fea-
12 tured in numerous magazines and architectural books. My commercial projects are often
13 massive in scale and detail.
14
15 On Friday, May 15, YR-1, I attended a firm social event, basically a happy hour from 5:30 to
16 7:30 p.m., at the Sunset Bar & Grill. Everyone calls it the Sunset. As one of the best-known
17 members of the firm, I like to make an appearance at these events to encourage camara-
18 derie and morale in the firm.
19
20 I left the office on May 15 at around 5:15 or 5:20 p.m. and drove down to the Sunset. I gave
21 one of the college interns, Riley Cameron, a ride to the event. We had a pretty good turn-
22 out for this particular event, and maybe twenty to twenty-five people were there when
23 we arrived. I socialized with my coworkers and clients at the event, as well as some other
24 Sunset patrons. I did not eat anything while at the Sunset because I had eaten a big lunch.
25 I am also training for a marathon in the fall and trying to stay away from bar food.
26
27 That being said, over the course of my time at the Sunset, I had two beers. I also paid for
28 Riley's beers. Riley had been working very hard on the A. T. Moore, Inc., project. Earlier
29 that day, the CEO of A. T. Moore had approved our plans for a new office building. I bought
30 Riley's beers as a thank you for his hard work on this project. I bought beers directly from
31 the bartender and put the beers on the bar tab that I opened with my credit card. As I said,
32 I only had two beers and the rest of the beers on that tab were purchased for Riley.
33
34 Officer Baldwin showed me the photo Riley had posted on Twitter with the caption
35 "Everyone partying, Peyton working." She asked me whose beers were in the photograph,
36 I told her that was me in the photo and that two of the beer bottles were mine. The other
37 bottles must have belonged to people who visited me at the table during the happy hour.
38
39 I was exhausted that evening and eager to be home. I started that day with an early five-
40 mile run. I spent the morning attending back-to-back meetings and, finally, spent all after-
41 noon correcting mistakes associates had made on some of my projects. It was a long and
42 tedious day. By 7:15 p.m., I had been going for more than thirteen hours.

1   I offered to give Riley a ride to his apartment. I have given him rides home in the past

2   when we work late. He lives between the firm and my house and not far from the Sunset,

3   so it was no trouble. The shortest route to Riley's apartment is up First or Second Avenue,

4   then down North Market and left on Eighth Avenue. Riley lives one block off of Eighth

5   Avenue on Arrow Road.

6

7   I had no reservations about driving. I did not feel drunk or even buzzed. It was about an

8   eight-minute drive from the Sunset to Riley's place, and in that time we talked about the

9   A. T. Moore project. During our conversation, Riley did not slur his words or act intoxi-

10   cated. Riley is a hard worker, but not the brightest student intern. I will not be offering him

11   an associate job when he graduates next month.

12

13   The drive through town was bumpy but uneventful. I think I came up First Avenue, took a

14   right on North Market Street, a left on Eighth Avenue, and a right on Arrow Road to Riley's

15   apartment. I don't always take the same route, but I am fairly sure that is the route I took last

16   night. Driving through that part of downtown is tough because of all of the potholes along

17   the side streets and down North Market Street. I stopped at every stop sign and red traffic

18   light that I encountered on the drive. I did not hear a horn honk during this trip, nor did I hit

19   another car. Riley and I talked for a minute outside of his house, and then I drove directly

20   home.

21

22   I pulled up to my house and parallel parked in a tight spot right in front. As I was getting

23   out of my car, a police officer approached me and asked me for my name and who had

24   been driving my car that night. I was cooperative. I told her my name and said that I was

25   the only person who drove my car that night. She asked me about some scratches that

26   were on the side of my car. I told her that I park in the garage at work and that I rubbed

27   against the rubbery part of a garage pylon a few days earlier. I had looked at the damage

28   in the dark garage, and it didn't look like much. I figured I would get it buffed out next time

29   I took my car into the shop. As I don't get in on the passenger side of my car, I just forgot

30   about it.

31

32   The officer then asked me if I had been drinking. I told her the truth. I told her that I had

33   two beers at my firm's happy hour. Even though I was cooperative and clearly not intoxi-

34   cated, she made me perform some sobriety tests. She seemed to be on a power trip. She

35   was very curt with me during the whole exchange. My cellphone rang during the tests.

36   The officer went nuts. She yelled at me to turn it off. I had no intention of answering the

37   call, but the officer still got angry.

38

39   First, she had me stand on one foot, close my eyes, and count to thirty. I asked her to

40   let me take my loafers off because they are slippery on the bottom and I didn't want to

41   perform badly because of my shoes. Also my legs and feet were killing me after my long

42   day. She reluctantly allowed me to remove my shoes, but when I started the first test,

43   my legs began to really hurt. Like I said, I am training for the Nita City marathon next fall,

44   and I ran fifteen miles the day before and five miles that morning. I had to drop my foot

45   around number six or seven, and again at sixteen, but I made it to thirty from there. I only

1   dropped my leg because I was sore from training. I told the officer about my training, but
2   she didn't seem to care.

3

4   Next, the officer had me close my eyes, put my head up, and touch my nose with my index
5   fingers. I was perfect on my first attempt with my right index finger, but I had some trouble
6   with my left hand. I am right-handed, so I missed with my left hand a couple times. I finally
7   got it on the third or fourth try with my left hand. I did not stumble or lose my balance dur-
8   ing this test. I just missed my nose with my left hand.

9

10 Finally, she asked me to walk heel-to-toe in a straight line, turn around, and walk the same
11 way back to my original place. I did fine on this test. I only wobbled slightly on the turn and
12 may have stepped out of line once, just slightly, on the return trip. The officer never told
13 me how fast to do this test, but she made some comment about it "taking a long time." I
14 asked to do it again, since she didn't tell me how fast, but she refused.

15

16 The officer then told me that she was arresting me for DUI and hit and run. I was shocked. I
17 did not know what she was talking about. I swore to her that I did not hit anyone. She told
18 me that I had sideswiped someone, causing slight damage to the side of some woman's
19 car and causing the woman to injure her hand. I told the officer that I would have stopped
20 if I had sideswiped a car, no matter how slight the damage. She told me the woman identi-
21 fied my car by the "Peyton & Dalton" sign on the door. I wonder if the woman identified
22 my car because I'm a deep pocket to sue. I am going to remove that sign as soon as I get
23 home. If the woman saw this happen, then the only explanation I have is that I did not
24 know that I hit her and possibly I thought I had gone over a pothole or some uneven pave-
25 ment. I would never knowingly leave the scene of an accident.

26

27 While I readily admit that I had two beers at the Sunset, there was no way I was drunk
28 when I was driving. I insisted that the officer give me a breath test to check my blood alco-
29 hol content. As I expected, it was only 0.06, which is below the legal limit.

30

31 She said that she was still charging me with DUI and hit and run and that I could tell the
32 judge all of my excuses. I can tell this is going to be just like that last time I dealt with the
33 police. When I was in college, I was in a restaurant and left in a hurry because I was ill. I
34 thought the person I was with was going to pay the bill, but he skipped out on the check.
35 I told the police and the court the truth, but I ended up with a misdemeanor conviction.

36

37 I could tell that Officer Baldwin just wanted her quota of arrests and didn't care about the
38 truth. This was especially true after she found the Sunset receipt in my pocket. I told her
39 that the seven drinks I paid for were not all for me, but I could tell she didn't believe me.

Signed and attested to this 16th day of May YR-1.

Exhibit 6

Photograph of Peyton & Dalton signage

Exhibit 6

Photograph of Peyton & Dalton stores

Exhibit 7

Peyton Driving Record

# *Nita Department of Motor Vehicles*	
Driver's Name: Jordan Peyton	DOB: 10/01/YR-36

Driving Record

Abstract As of 01/01/YR-0

Incident Date	Description	Disposition
7/4/YR-3	Charged: Reckless Driving	9/1/YR-3: Reduced—Pled G to Speeding 10–14 MPH over limit

This signature and seal is to certify that this is an accurate copy of the Driving Record of Jordan Peyton as of the date indicated above and that all information contained within this report is true.

Jim Smithfield
DMV Clerk

State Department of
Motor Vehicles

		DOB: 10/01/YR-36

Incident Date	Description	Disposition

Exhibit 8

Peyton Criminal Record

Circuit Court of the City of Nita, State of Nita

Defendant's Name: Jordan Peyton	DOB: 10/01/YR-36

Criminal Record
As of 01/01/YR-0

Incident Date	Charge	Disposition
6/1/YR-12	Larceny Under $300 (misdemeanor)	8/4/YR-12: Pled NG/Found G Petit Larceny Sentenced thirty days jail/all suspended—conditioned on uniform good behavior for one year

This signature and seal is to certify that this is an accurate copy of the entire Criminal Record of Jordan Peyton on file at the Circuit Court of the City of Nita, and that all information contained within this report is true.

Clerk of the Court

Exhibit 9

PAGE 1 OF 2

STATE OF NITA

POLICE REPORT

DATE OF INCIDENT OCCURRENCE	TIME	NCIC NUMBER	OFFICER ID NUMBER	CASE NUMBER
05-15-YR-1	**7:35 p.m.**	**46768**	**679**	**CR-1112**

"X" ONE	"X" ONE	TYPE SUPPLEMENTAL ("X" APPLICABLE)		
☐ NARRATIVE	☒ CRIMINAL REPORT	☐ COLLISION UPDATE	☐ FATAL	☒ HIT AND RUN
☒ SUPPLEMENTAL	☐ OTHER	☐ SCHOOL BUS	☐ OTHER	

SUBJECT	REPORTING DISTRICT/BEAT	CITATION NUMBER
Arrest of Jordan Peyton	**2nd Dist.**	**N/A**

NARRATIVE:

This is a supplemental report.

At the end of my twelve-hour shift on May 16, YR-1 at approximately 7:00 a.m., I photographed Taylor Addison's silver Trailblazer. When I arrived at the intersection of Second Avenue and North Market Street, the vehicle was in the same position it had been the evening before. As the victim had been transported to the hospital by ambulance, her vehicle appeared to have remained undisturbed all night. The window was even in the down position as it had been the evening before. The paper coffee cup was no longer on the scene. I photographed the vehicle from multiple angles. Photographs are attached to this report.

I collected paint scrapings from the point of impact on the victim's vehicle and secured them in an evidence envelope. On close observation, I could see that the black plastic of the bumper could be seen through the paint in places. I did not observe any paint color other than silver.

On May 16, YR-1, at approximately 7:00 p.m., I proceeded to the residence of Jordan Peyton. Her silver Mercedes was not where it had been parked the night before. I was unable to locate her vehicle on that day. A few days later, I located her vehicle in the parking garage of her office building. The Peyton & Dalton magnetic sign had been removed from the passenger side door. Pursuant to the search warrant I had obtained, I photographed the damage to her vehicle and collected paint scrapings from the scratched area. I secured the scrapings in an evidence envelope. On close observation, I could see what I believed to be black rubber

State of Nita	
POLICE REPORT	PAGE 2 OF 2

transfer marks that could have come from either the black rubber strip on the base of Addison's front bumper or possibly the black strip on the side of Addison's vehicle. I did not observe any paint color other than silver. Photographs are attached to this report.

Note that I included an additional copy of one of the Mercedes photographs and one of the Trailblazer photographs that include a superimposed ruler demonstrating the height of some of the scratches. As you can see from where the rulers line up with the scratchs—there are a few points where the sratches on the cars line up perfectly.

Attached is a close-to-scale diagram of the intersection of Second Avenue and North Market Street. I observed a number of potholes, fist-sized dislodged chunks of pavement, and generally poor road conditions on Second Avenue in the blocks directly east of North Market Street; however, there are no potholes or debris within fifteen (15) feet of the location of Addison's vehicle. I reported the poor road conditions to the Nita Department of Transportation.

Tests on the paint scrapings were inconclusive. No affirmative match could be made between the two vehicles. According to the lab, the scrapings from both vehicles appeared to contain only paint consistent with the car from which the scrapings were collected.

PREPARERS NAME, RANK, AND DIVISION	DATE
BALDWIN, LEE, OFFICER, SECOND DISTRICT PATROL	**05-25-YR-1**

Exhibit 10

Peyton Vehicle Registration

NITA Department of Motor Vehicles	
Driver's Name: Jordan Peyton	DOB: 10/01/YR-36

Vehicle Registration
As of 01/01/YR-0

Make	Model	Year	License Tag #
Mercedes-Benz	E350/4 door	YR-2	PNDRGR8

This signature and seal is to certify that this is an accurate copy of the Vehicle Registration Information of Jordan Peyton as of the date indicted above and that all information contained within this report is true.

Jim Smithfield
DMV Clerk

Exhibit 11

Search Warrant and Inventory Sheet

THE CIRCUIT COURT FOR THE CITY OF NITA

In the Matter of the Search of,   )
the silver Mercedes Benz belonging to   )
Jordan Peyton, residing at   )   Case No. CR 1112
1313 Randolph Road   )
Nita City, 12345   )

SEARCH AND SEIZURE WARRANT

To: Any authorized law enforcement officer

An application by a law enforcement officer or an attorney for the government requests the search of the following property located in the City of Nita:

The YR-2 silver Mercedes-Benz C-Class series 4-door sedan belonging to Jordan Peyton of 1313 Randolph Road, Nita City, 12345, specifically, to collect paint samples from the vehicles for further testing and analysis in a driving under the influence and hit and run investigation.

I find that the affidavit(s), or any recorded testimony, establish probable cause to search and seize the property described above, and that such search will reveal:

That Peyton's Mercedes struck the Victim's Chevy Trailblazer; the paint samples should match paint samples taken from the damaged area of the Victim's Chevy Trailblazer because either the paint from the Victim's vehicle transferred onto Peyton's vehicle or the paint from Peyton's vehicle transferred onto the Victim's vehicle during the collision.

YOU ARE COMMANDED to execute this warrant on or before **May 30, YR-1** *(not to exceed 14 days*

☒ in the daytime 6:00 a.m. to 10:00 p.m.   ☐ at any time in the day or night because good
                                                cause has been established.

Unless delayed notice is authorized below, you must give a copy of the warrant and a receipt for the property taken to the person from whom, or from whose premises, the property was taken, or leave the copy and receipt at the place where the property was taken.

The officer executing this warrant, or an officer present during the execution of the warrant, must prepare an inventory as required by law and promptly return this warrant and inventory to authorizing judge.

Date and time issued: _____   _____

                                                  Judge's Signature

City and State: _____   _____

                                                  Printed name and official title

Return

Case No.:	Date and time warrant executed:	Copy of warrant and inventory left with:
CP-1112	5/16/YR1 7:00 PM	

Inventory made in the presence of:

Inventory of the property taken and name of any person(s) seized:

Paint scrapings from the scratched area, rear end of the passenger side, of Jordan Peyton's silver Mercedes with plate number __PNDRGR8__ .

Certification

I declare under penalty of perjury that this inventory is correct and was returned along with the original warrant to the designated judge.

Date: __5/16/YR1__

Officer Lee Baldwin
Executing officer's signature

Office Lee Baldwin, Second District Patrol
Printed name and title

Exhibit 12

Intersection Diagram

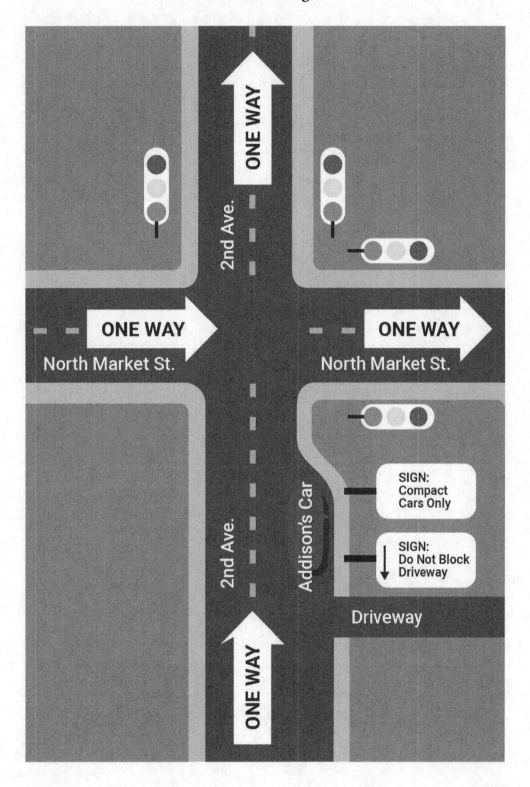

Exhibit 12

Intersection Diagram

Exhibit 13

Body Camera Video*

*To view this video, please visit the following site:

https://stetson.ensemblevideo.com/Watch/b7XYp39Q

Exhibit 14

Photograph of Addison Vehicle* (Rear View 1)

*To view images in color, please visit our digital download site at:

http://bit.ly/1P20Jea
Password: Peyton3

Exhibit 15

Photograph of Addison Vehicle (Rear View 2)

Exhibit 16

Photograph of Addison Vehicle (Damage)

Exhibit 16

Photograph of Addition Vehicle Damage

Exhibit 17

Photograph of Peyton Vehicle (Damage)

Exhibit 17

Photograph of Figure Vehicle Damage

Exhibit 18

Photograph of Measured Scratches on Peyton Vehicle
Compared to Addison Vehicle

STATEMENT OF RILEY CAMERON

1   Officer Baldwin asked me to write this statement and sign it as a true and accurate account
2   of what happened during my ride home from the happy hour on May 15, YR-1. My name
3   is Riley Cameron. I am twenty-one years old. I live on Arrow Road in Nita City, and I am an
4   intern at the architecture firm of Peyton & Dalton. I go to Nita State University and am in
5   my final year studying architecture. I started working at Peyton & Dalton in May of YR-2
6   and hope to be hired as an associate after my graduation next month.
7

8   During my time as an intern, I have participated in a number of social outings with mem-
9   bers of the firm. There would often be alcohol consumed at these events, though I cannot
10   remember an instance in which Ms. Peyton or anyone was drunk or disorderly. At these
11   functions, Ms. Peyton would have a drink or two, at the most, and sometimes she would
12   buy me a few drinks or a meal. She is a very generous person.
13

14   On Friday, May 15, YR-1, Ms. Peyton received good news that A. T. Moore, Inc., a real
15   estate development company and one of our big clients, approved our design plans for a
16   large office building in downtown Nita City. I worked on these plans with Ms. Peyton for
17   months. At around 5:00 p.m. that evening, Ms. Peyton came to my cubicle and gave me
18   the news in person. She offered to buy me a few drinks at the firm happy hour that evening
19   as a way of thanking me for my hard work on the plans.
20

21   Ms. Peyton and I rode together to the firm happy hour at the Sunset. We arrived around
22   5:30 or 5:45 p.m. I spent some of my time by the end of the bar, talking with a group of
23   interns. When I ate my burger, I sat at one of the tables with Ms. Peyton but she worked
24   the whole time on her phone.
25

26   During the course of the event, Ms. Peyton bought me a few beers as a thank you for my
27   work on the A. T. Moore project. I do not remember specifically how many she bought me,
28   but I think it was four. I also ordered myself a beer and a cheeseburger and fries like I men-
29   tioned. I paid the bartender directly in cash for the additional beer and food. I think I had
30   maybe five beers total at the event. I certainly wasn't drunk. Five beers really do not have
31   much of an effect on me. I am a college student, so I socialize and drink a lot of beer. Plus,
32   I ate a big cheeseburger and fries that really diluted the effect of the alcohol.
33

34   Around 7:20 p.m., Ms. Peyton offered to give me a ride home. I had plans for later that
35   night and I do not have a car, so I accepted her offer.
36

37   I know that Ms. Peyton has been charged with DUI. Ms. Peyton was not drunk or even
38   buzzed when she was driving me home. We had a normal conversation about the A. T.
39   Moore project, and she was not slurring her words. The trip from the Sunset to my apart-
40   ment probably took about five to ten minutes, though I really cannot remember exactly.
41   The trip was routine. I do not remember anything unusual happening. I am not sure which

1 route through downtown she took, but I remember commenting on the need for road
2 repair because it was a bumpy ride.
3
4 Officer Baldwin showed me the tweet that I sent out right when I got home on May 15,
5 YR-1. Yes, I wrote that tweet. When I said, "home safely—barely," I was referring to the
6 fact that Ms. Peyton is known for driving fast and riding up on other cars' bumpers. I was
7 just making a joke. She wasn't driving erratically or fast that night. The #hotrod is a run-
8 ning joke between the associates. I also posted a photo in that tweet with the caption
9 "Everyone partying, Peyton working." Officer Baldwin asked me whose beers were in the
10 photograph, I told her I didn't know but everyone at the table had been drinking Heineken.
11
12 Ms. Peyton called me into her office a few days after the happy hour and told me that
13 she had been charged with hitting a car in the intersection of Second Avenue and North
14 Market Street on the way to my place. There is no way she could have hit a car without me
15 knowing it. I don't know what street we took to North Market Street. It could have been
16 First or Second.
17
18 It is worth noting, I remember seeing scratches on the passenger side of her car when I got
19 in her car to leave the happy hour.
20
21 There must be some kind of mistake. Ms. Peyton would never leave the scene of a crime.
22 She is the most honest person I know. Everyone at the firm and people in the architecture
23 community know that Ms. Peyton is honest—almost to a fault—because she tells clients
24 exactly what they can expect in project costs rather than underestimating costs like the
25 rest of the firms in the industry. An associate at the firm told me that Ms. Peyton has lost
26 lucrative jobs because she was too honest with prospective clients. I have nothing further.

Signed and attested to this 20th day of May YR-1.

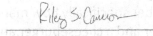

Exhibit 19

Riley Cameron Tweets

THE PEOPLE OF   )
 THE STATE OF NITA   )
)
  v.   )   Case No. CR 1112
)
JORDAN PEYTON   )
)
 Defendant.   )

FELONY HIT AND RUN PRELIMINARY HEARING TRANSCRIPT

Witness: Taylor Addison

Direct Examination by State's Counsel:

1	Q:	Please state your name for the record.
2	A:	Taylor Addison.
3	Q:	What is your address?
4	A:	447 Lockney Drive, Jamesburg, in the State of Columbia.
5	Q:	What is your occupation?
6	A:	I used to be a carpenter, but I have been out of work since Ms. Peyton hit my car.

7 Defense: I object to Ms. Addison's representation that Ms. Peyton hit her car. I do not
8   believe that Ms. Addison is able to identify the driver of the car that hit her.
9   I object to her characterization.

10 Judge: Overruled. You can explore that issue on cross-examination.

11 Q: Let's talk about the incident. When did it occur?

12 A: May 15, YR-1.

13 Q: Where did it occur?

14 A: At the intersection of Second Avenue and North Market Street. I was parked along the
15   curb in the last space on Second Avenue before that intersection.

16 Q: What happened?

17 A: I was early for a meeting with a potential client, who was planning some storefront
18   renovations. He wanted me to come by at 8:00 p.m., so I got a cup of black coffee and

1   an apple pie from the drive-thru a few blocks from the client's store. That was at about

2   7:30 p.m. I parked my car on the side of Second Avenue, took off my seat belt, and ate

3   my apple pie. The coffee was extremely hot, so I took off the lid to let it cool. At approxi-

4   mately 7:35 p.m., I picked up the coffee in my left hand and looked down at some papers

5   in my lap.

6   Q: What happened next?

7   A: I sensed a light-colored car moving past me on my left. I didn't think anything of it until,

8   all of a sudden, my car lurched to the right. The steaming hot coffee sloshed over the

9   rim of the cup and poured over my left hand. I threw the cup out my open car window.

10   I was in so much pain. I grabbed some napkins from the passenger seat and tried to

11   get the coffee off my hand. Once I got the spill under control, I looked up and saw a

12   silver Mercedes heading slowly down North Market Street away from the scene. I think

13   the Mercedes slowed down to stop at the light, hit my car, and then got the green and

14   turned right on North Market.

15   Q: What else could you see?

16   A: I saw two people in the Mercedes. I couldn't see the driver's face because she was al-

17   ready on North Market heading north when I was finally able to focus on her through

18   the pain.

19   Defense: I object to Ms. Addison's representation that a woman was driving the Mer-

20   cedes. She just testified that she could not see the driver's face. I object to

21   her characterization.

22   Judge: Sustained. Ms. Addison, please refrain from testifying to things that you do

23   not have firsthand knowledge of.

24   Q: What happened next?

25   A: I beeped my horn a few times with my right hand, but the Mercedes did not stop.

26   Q: Were there any unique characteristics about this Mercedes?

27   A: Yes. It has a sign on the passenger side door for the architecture firm of Peyton & Dalton.

28   Q: What do you know about Peyton & Dalton?

29   A: I know they are a successful residential and commercial architecture firm. I did some

30   work on a renovation project for them a few years back. It was a small job so I really

31   didn't get to know any of the employees.

32   Q: What happened next?

33   A: Well, as soon as the Mercedes drove away, I called 911 to report the hit and run. Officer

34   Baldwin arrived within a few minutes.

35   Q: What did Officer Baldwin do when she arrived?

1　A:　She interviewed me.

2　Q:　What kind of car were you driving that day?

3　A:　A silver Chevy Trailblazer.

4　Q:　Was there any damage to your front left bumper before the incident you just
5　　　described?

6　A:　No. The bumper was in perfect shape before Ms. Peyton hit me.

7　Defense:　　I renew my objection to Ms. Addison's speculation that Ms. Peyton was the
8　　　　　　driver of the car that hit her.

9　Judge:　　Sustained. Ms. Addison, please do not make me instruct you again to refrain
10　　　　　from testifying to things that you do not have firsthand knowledge of.

11　Q:　What did the bumper look like after the incident?

12　A:　There were a bunch of scratches on the front driver's side corner of the bumper.

13　Q:　After the incident, did you have to bring your car in for repairs?

14　A:　Yes, I did. I took the car to the Johnson Brothers. I have known them for a while and know
15　　　that they are pretty honest guys, so that is where I always bring my car if it needs to be
16　　　fixed.

17　Q:　And did they give you a receipt for the repair work?

18　A:　Yes, they did.

19　Q:　How much did it cost to fix your bumper?

20　A:　The total cost was $480.

21　Q:　Ms. Addison, you testified earlier that when the coffee spilled it burned your hand. Can
22　　　you tell the judge about your injury?

23　A:　Yes. I suffered first- and second-degree burns on my left hand and wrist. The coffee was
24　　　so hot it caused my hand to swell and the skin to turn a deep red and blister in spots. It
25　　　was extremely painful.

26　Q:　Ms. Addison, I am showing you a photograph that has been marked as State's Exhibit 20.
27　　　Can you tell the judge what is depicted in this photograph?

28　A:　Yes, this is a photograph that was taken by the medical staff in the emergency room
29　　　where I was admitted on the evening of May 15, YR-1. That is exactly what my hand and
30　　　wrist looked like within an hour or so of the coffee spill.

31　Q:　I move to admit State's Exhibit 20 in evidence.

32　Judge:　　Admitted.

1   Q: Have you healed from the injury?

2   A: Mostly, but the new skin on my hand is still sensitive to the sun and hot and cold tem-
3   peratures. Since I am left-handed, my injury is constantly coming in touch with things
4   and each touch sends a slight ting of pain up the back of my hand.

5   Q: Did the driver of the silver Mercedes stop and talk to you after hitting your car?

6   A: No.

7   Q: I have nothing further.

8   **Cross-Examination by Defense Counsel:**

9   Q: Your car was parked on Second Avenue?

10   A: Yes.

11   Q: Your car was parked on the right side of the street facing North Market Street?

12   A: Yes.

13   Q: In the area around where you parked, there are signs on the sides of Second Avenue
14   that indicate the parking regulations in that area?

15   A: I think so.

16   Q: In fact, there were signs right next to where you parked your car?

17   A: I think so.

18   Q: There was a sign that indicated that only compact cars should park in the space your car
19   was parked in?

20   A: The officer did point that out to me, but said she was not going to give me a citation for
21   it.

22   Q: Your Trailblazer is not a compact car, correct?

23   A: No.

24   Q: You did not see the Mercedes actually strike your car, did you?

25   A: No, but I felt it and I know that the car that struck my car was white or silver. I could see
26   the light color out of the corner of my eye.

27   Q: You did not see the Mercedes on Second Avenue?

28   A: I think I did. Like I said, I could see a light-colored car hit me, but I can't say for sure it
29   was the Mercedes. However, the Mercedes was the only light-colored car near me when
30   I looked up.

31   Q: You did not follow the Mercedes?

1 A: No. I was in shock and pain.

2 Q: After you got the burn under control and looked up, the Mercedes was actually on North
3   Market, correct?

4 A: Yes.

5 Q: You didn't see the Mercedes turn from Second to North Market, did you?

6 A: I didn't have to see it. It was evident because the Mercedes was going slowly as if it had
7   just turned from Second Avenue on to North Market. It was going much slower than the
8   other cars on North Market.

9 Q: And there were other cars on North Market?

10 A: Yes, but I don't recall any of them being light colored.

11 Q: And there were other cars on Second Avenue?

12 A: I think there were other cars, I just can't identify them, but there weren't any other cars
13   between mine and the Mercedes.

14 Q: You know that Peyton & Dalton is a successful residential and commercial architecture
15   firm?

16 A: Yes.

17 Q: And you know that means that the partners in the firm are very wealthy?

18 Prosecutor: Irrelevant.

19 Judge: Sustained.

20 Q: Ms. Addison do you intend to sue Ms. Peyton in civil court for the injuries you received
21   from this accident?

22 A: Absolutely. I plan to sue her after the criminal charges are resolved.

23 Defense: I have nothing further.

I certify that the foregoing document is a true and accurate transcription of Taylor Addison's preliminary hearing testimony, which was given under oath, on July 15, YR-1, in the case of State v. Jordan Peyton in the District Court, Nita City, Nita.

Certified by:

John Allan Michael

John Allan Michael
Court Reporter
Commission number: 6548
My Commission expires: December 30, YR-0

Exhibit 20

Photographs of Addison Hand Injury*

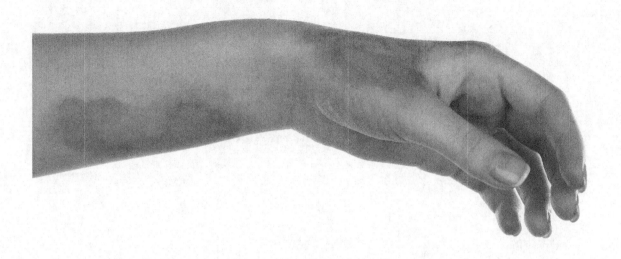

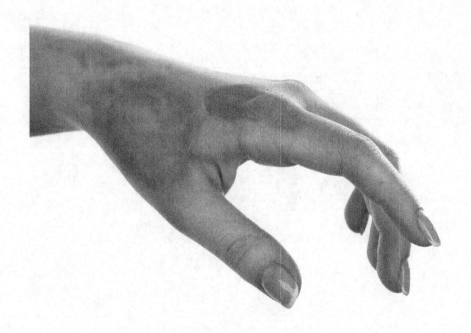

*To view images in color, please visit our digital download site at:

http://bit.ly/1P20Jea
Password: Peyton3

Exhibit 21

Addison Vehicle Repair Receipt

Johnson Brothers Auto Collision Experts
"It's broken—so fix it"

Damage Description: Front driver's side bumper scratched	**Date: 05/19/YR-1**
Repair Description Replaced front bumper	**Time 3:30 PM**

Repair Details

Parts		
Parts		
	New Front Bumper	$350
Labor ($100/hour)		
	1 hour	$100
Subtotal		$450
Sales Tax:		$30
Total:		**$480**
Payment Received: Check # 1476		**$480**
Balance Due		**$0**

IN THE CIRCUIT COURT FOR
THE CITY OF NITA

THE PEOPLE OF	)
THE STATE OF NITA	)
	)
v.	) Case No. CR 1112
	)
JORDAN PEYTON	)
	)
Defendant.	)

FELONY HIT AND RUN
PRELIMINARY HEARING TRANSCRIPT

Witness: Pat Carter

Direct Examination by State's Counsel:

1 Q: Please state your name, address, and occupation for the record.

2 A: My name is Pat Carter. I live at 335 Sylvan Lake Road in Nita City. I am currently an assis-
3 tant manager and bartender at the Sunset Bar & Grill.

4 Q: How long have you worked at the Sunset Bar & Grill?

5 A: Ten years.

6 Q: And is there any training associated with your positions?

7 A: Yes. I have a bachelor degree from Southern Nita University in Hotel and Restaurant
8 Management, and I have taken courses on bartending and bar management.

9 Q: What did you learn in your bartending and bar management courses?

10 A: Well, I learned how to mix drinks and deal with customers. I also learned how to spot
11 and deal with intoxicated individuals, as well as all of the business procedures for run-
12 ning a restaurant and bar.

13 Q: Why is it important to learn how to spot and deal with intoxicated patrons?

14 A: Well, you need to know when to stop serving them for their own safety and the safety
15 and enjoyment of the other patrons.

16 Q: What are the signs that someone is intoxicated?

17 A: Intoxicated people slur their words, have glassy and bloodshot eyes, are unsteady on
18 their feet, and often have trouble following simple instructions such as "you need to
19 leave the bar now."

1   Q: What types of things are involved with running the bar at Sunset?

2   A: Well, on nights that I work, I am responsible for handling the nightly receipts.

3   Q: What do you mean by "receipts"?

4   A: Receipts are the printouts of how the patrons' orders were paid. For example, a receipt
5   will show what was ordered and if the person paid cash or credit. If a person paid by
6   credit, it will show the name, order, date, amount paid, and the last four digits of the
7   credit card.

8   Q: How are the credit card receipts handled?

9   A: I collect all of the credit card receipts at the end of the night and make a notation on the
10   balance sheets. Then I collect the money and put it in the safe for the night. I have to
11   make sure we were paid for everything we served, so the total of credit card sales and
12   cash should equal the amount sold that night.

13   Q: How long do you keep the credit card receipts?

14   A: Two years, as required by state law.

15   Q: Where are they kept?

16   A: In the office file cabinet.

17   Q: Why do you keep the receipts?

18   A: Well, it's company policy to keep them for at least two years to properly report them
19   for business purposes and also to settle any disputed charges that may arise with credit
20   card companies or patrons.

21   Q: Did you review anything before testifying here?

22   A: Yes, I looked at the receipts from May 15, YR-1.

23   Q: Why May 15, YR-1?

24   A: Because you asked me to.

25   Q: Did you work at the Sunset on May 15, YR-1?

26   A: Yes.

27   Q: How do you remember that you worked that day?

28   A: Easy. It was my birthday. I was scheduled to have the night off, but Peyton & Dalton had
29   a social event scheduled and the other two bartenders were unavailable. I wasn't happy
30   about being there, but I was there.

31   Q: Let the record reflect that I am showing defense counsel what has been marked as
32   State's Exhibit 22. Your Honor, may I approach the witness?

1   Judge: Yes, you may.

2   Q: Mr. Carter, can you identify State's Exhibit 22?

3   A: Yes. It is Jordan Peyton's bar receipt from May 15, YR-1.

4   Q: How do you know what it is?

5   A: It has the Sunset logo on the top and contains the date, her name, and my name as the
6   server.

7   Q: Is this one of the receipts you were referring to earlier in your testimony?

8   A: Yes. This is a credit card receipt from May 15, YR-1. I collected it with all of the other
9   receipts from that night and retained it in our files for tax and credit card purchase veri-
10   fication purposes.

11 Q: Is that your regular business procedure?

12 A: Yes.

13 Q: Has this document been modified in any way since May 15, YR-1?

14 A: No. It is the original.

15 Prosecutor: Your Honor, I move for admission of State's Exhibit 22 into evidence.

16 Defense: I object to this receipt on the grounds that there is a double layer of hearsay.
17   Although it appears to satisfy the business records exception, it still contains
18   notations apparently made by a computer system regarding the number of
19   beers ordered and paid for on this receipt. There is no way for the defendant
20   to cross-examine the computer to ensure the reliability of this information.

21 Judge: Objection overruled. The receipt is admitted.

22 Q: What information is contained on the receipt?

23 A: The Sunset logo, date of May 15, YR-1, and Jordan Peyton's name, signature, and the last
24   four digits of the credit card number of the card she used. The receipt also has my name
25   listed as the server. It shows that she paid for seven imported bottled beers that night,
26   and she paid sometime after the receipt was printed at 7:18 p.m.

27 Q: Who is Jordan Peyton?

28 A: She is the boss over at Peyton & Dalton.

29 Q: How do you know her?

30 A: She comes into the Sunset four or five times a month. Sometimes she is alone, and other
31   times with friends. She also comes when Peyton & Dalton has events.

32 Q: Was she present at the social event on May 15, YR-1?

1   A: Yes.

2   Q: Do you personally recall if she was drinking?

3   A: Yes, I remember serving her some beers.

4   Q: How many beers did you give her?

5   A: Well, she ordered seven beers, so I served her seven.

6   Prosecutor: No further questions.

7   **Cross-Examination by Defense Counsel:**

8   Q: You stated she ordered seven beers; did you see her drink any of them?

9   A: Well, not exactly. The bar was pretty packed, so I didn't see her actually drink any of the
10   beers.

11   Q: As a matter of fact, it is common practice for people to buy drinks for other people, isn't
12   that correct?

13   A: Yes, that's a pretty common thing to do.

14   Q: Ms. Peyton did not slur her words on May 15, did she?

15   A: Not that I recall.

16   Q: She did not have trouble walking to or from the bar?

17   A: Not that I recall.

18   Q: Never appeared intoxicated at all, in fact?

19   A: Not that I recall.

20   Q: You did not prohibit Ms. Peyton from ordering alcohol on May 15, YR-1, did you?

21   A: No.

22   Q: You never cut her off?

23   A: No.

24   Q: You did not cut anyone off on May 15, YR-1, did you?

25   A: I don't remember.

26   Q: Mr. Carter, do you know Riley Cameron?

27   Prosecution: Objection. Outside the scope.

28   Judge: Sustained.

I certify that the foregoing document is a true and accurate transcription of Pat Carter's preliminary hearing testimony, which was given under oath, on July 15, YR-1, in the case of State v. Jordan Peyton in the District Court, Nita City, Nita.

Certified by:

John Allan Michael

John Allan Michael
Court Reporter
Commission number: 6548
My Commission expires: December 30, YR-0

Exhibit 22

Sunset Bar & Grill Receipt (signed copy)

Sunset Bar & Grill

Your Neighborhood Bar

****

Server: Pat Carter
Date: May 15, YR-1
Time: 7:18 p.m.

. . . .

ORDER:

7 Imported Bottle Beer
@ 5.00 . . . . $35.00

Subtotal $35.00

Tax (10%) . . $03.50

Total $38.50

****

Card: xxxx xxxx xxxx 2398

Tip ___6.00___

Total ___44.50___

___Jordan Peyton___
Jordan Peyton

****

THANK YOU!
PLEASE COME AGAIN

Merchant Copy

Exhibit 23

PAGE 1 OF 1

STATE OF NITA

POLICE REPORT

DATE OF INCIDENT OCCURRENCE	TIME	NCIC NUMBER	OFFICER ID NUMBER	CASE NUMBER
05-15-YR-1	**7:35 p.m.**	**46768**	**679**	**CR-1112**

"X" ONE	"X" ONE	TYPE SUPPLEMENTAL ("X" APPLICABLE)		
☐ NARRATIVE	☒ CRIMINAL REPORT	☐ COLLISION UPDATE	☐ FATAL	☒ HIT AND RUN
☒ SUPPLEMENTAL	☐ OTHER	☐ SCHOOL BUS	☐ OTHER	

SUBJECT	REPORTING DISTRICT/BEAT	CITATION NUMBER
Arrest of Jordan Peyton	**2nd Dist.**	**N/A**

NARRATIVE:

This is a supplemental report.

On July 25, YR-1, Pat Carter was killed in a fire at the Sunset Bar & Grill. News article is attached to this report.

On August 1, YR-1, I contacted the receptionist at Peyton & Dalton to check the status of Riley Cameron's employment with the firm. The receptionist stated that Mr. Cameron was not hired as an associate of the firm in June YR-1. She volunteered that after Mr. Cameron was let go from Peyton & Dalton in the summer of YR-1, he took an associate position with the competing architecture firm of Caston Architectural Designs.

PREPARERS NAME, RANK, AND DIVISION	DATE
BALDWIN, LEE, OFFICER, SECOND DISTRICT PATROL	**08-01-YR-1**

Exhibit 24

July 26, YR-1

NITA CITY POST
Arson Suspected Cause of
Sunset Bar & Grill Fire

By: Jane Dabber

The Sunset Bar & Grill, 1301 Brentwood Road in Nita City, was set ablaze after closing time last night, according to investigators. The Nita City Fire Department now suspects the fire to be the result of an arsonist.

The Sunset Bar & Grill was completely destroyed in the blaze. Nothing was salvable, including all of the furniture, inventory, and business records. During an interview, the owner of Sunset Bar & Grill sadly stated, "This is a tragic occurrence, and although I have considered it, I do not plan on rebuilding the Sunset Bar & Grill."

The tragic fire not only annihilated the restaurant, but it took two lives. One has been identified as Pat Carter, 34, assistant manager and long-time bartender of the Sunset Bar & Grill. The second victim has yet to be identified. The owner addressed his sorrow for the loss of a well-respected and hard-working employee, "Pat will be greatly missed and remembered for his exceptional customer service and kind smile." The Nita City Police Department continues to investigate the fire, as there are no suspects yet. If you have any information on this fire, please contact the Nita City Police Department.

Exhibit 25

Email from Defense Attorney Re: Diagrams

From:	Amal Jagetta <a.jagetta@defenselawyers.nita>
Sent:	Jun 20, YR-1 11:33 AM
To:	exhibits <exhibits@nitastateattorneygeneral.nita>
Subject:	State v. Peyton—street diagrams
Attachments:	Streetdiag1.jpg, Streetdiag2.jpg

Enclosed is a close-to-scale diagram, drafted by my paralegal, illustrating the route Ms. Peyton took from the Sunset, up First Avenue, and on to the passenger's apartment.

In the interest of an efficient resolution of this case at trial, we provide this potential trial exhibit in advance of trial.

Map from Sunset Grill to Riley Cameron's Apartment (with route marked)

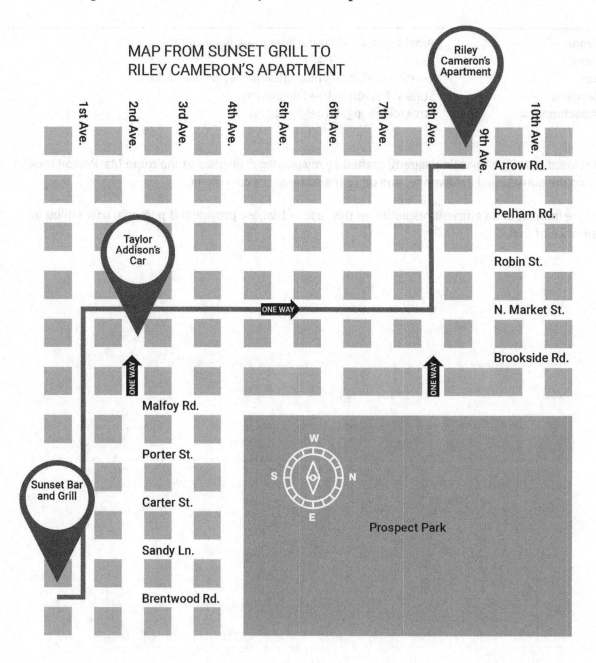

Map from Sunset Grill to Riley Cameron's Apartment (without route marked)

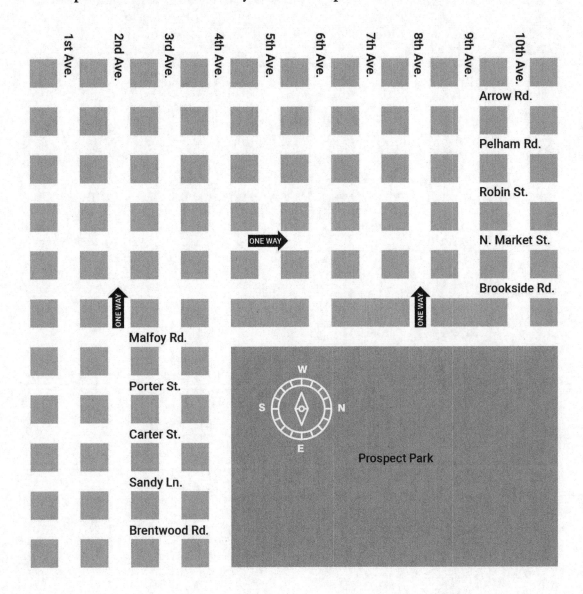

EXPERT WITNESS TESTIMONY

KIPPER WILLIAMS, MD

Nita State University Hospital

2187 University Avenue

Nita City, Nita 81287

Phone: 719-555-3827 Email: kwilliams@nsuh.nita

August 20, YR-1

Re: Jordan Peyton Driving Under the Influence and Hit and Run

Dear Assistant State's Attorney:

Per your request, I have reviewed the Jordan Peyton police case file and Intoxilyzer test results to determine the likely BAC of Ms. Peyton at the time she struck the victim's car. In my expert opinion and to a reasonable degree of medical certainty, Ms. Peyton's BAC was likely between 0.09 and 0.11 at the time of the incident.

Introduction

As we have never worked together on a case, I have attached my CV for your reference. As you can see from my CV, I am uniquely qualified to analyze cases such as this one. I am presently a resident physician at Nita State University Hospital. Last year, I received my MD from Xavier University School of Medicine in Aruba. I earned a BS in criminal justice from Nita State University. After graduating from college, I attended the Nita State Police Academy and then worked as a state trooper for six years. During my years on the force, I was certified to administer blood alcohol tests using the Intoxilyzer. During my last few years as a state trooper, I was certified as an instructor to teach other officers the proper procedures for administrating Intoxilyzer tests. As a state trooper, I administered hundreds of Intoxilyzer tests and testified in approximately eighty DUI cases as a witness police officer for the State.

I have consulted with the State on a number of DUI cases since my graduation from medical school, but the defendants in those cases pled guilty, so I was not required to testify in court. I have never assisted a defendant in a DUI case or testified in court as a medical expert.

Blood Alcohol Content

On average, it takes approximately one hour for the average human body to metabolize one alcoholic drink. In this context, one drink equals a five-ounce glass of wine, twelve-ounce beer, or one-and-a-half ounce shot of liquor.

According to the police report, the defendant stated that she consumed two beers between 5:30 and 7:30 p.m. and had not eaten anything since lunch. An empty stomach will speed up the alcohol absorption rate. This means that Ms. Peyton's BAC would reach its peak more quickly than it would have if she had a full stomach. I have attached a bell curve diagram to generally illustrate this process.

To a reasonable degree of medical certainty, I believe that Ms. Peyton was near the peak of her BAC at the time she was driving and down the decreasing side on the bell curve when she submitted her sample to the Intoxilyzer. Extrapolating backward from the time of her test, I would say that her BAC at the time she was driving was between 0.09 and 0.11.

In addition, it is highly unlikely that the defendant is telling the truth about the amount of alcohol she consumed. By the time she was given the Intoxilyzer test, approximately two and a half hours had passed since her last drink of alcohol. There is no possible way that she could have had only two beers between 5:30 and 7:30 p.m. and still register a 0.06 at 9:30 p.m.

It is highly likely that the defendant consumed four to six beers at the event. This conclusion is supported by the officer's observations of the defendant outside her residence approximately thirty minutes after consuming her last drink. As reported by the officer, Ms. Peyton had glassy and bloodshot eyes. Consumption of two beers over a two-hour period is not likely to manifest itself in glassy and bloodshot eyes; however, consumption of four to six beers in that time period would likely have that effect. The officer's observations of Ms. Peyton during the field sobriety tests also support the conclusion that Ms. Peyton was under the influence of alcohol to a degree consistent with her consumption of four to six beers rather than two beers as she claimed.

Conclusion

As I have stated above, I believe that Ms. Peyton had a BAC between 0.09 and 0.11 when she was driving on May 15, YR-1. At a BAC in this range, Ms. Peyton's motor skills, vision, and judgment would be impaired to a degree that would make it unsafe for her to operate a motor vehicle. In fact, medical studies have shown that any BAC above 0.08 would likely indicate that she was impaired to the point that she could not operate a motor vehicle safely.

I hope this information assists with your successful prosecution of Ms. Peyton. If I can help further, please do not hesitate to contact me. As I told you on the phone, I will not charge the State for my services in this case as I feel it is my civic duty.

Sincerely,

Kipper Williams, MD

Bell Curve Chart According to Dr. Kipper Williams

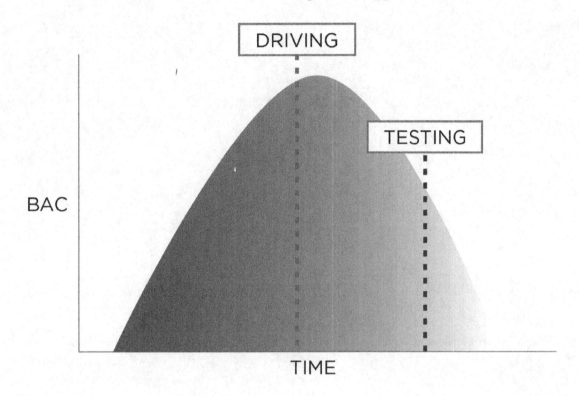

KIPPER WILLIAMS, MD, CURRICULUM VITAE

EDUCATION

YR-5 to YR-1	Xavier University School of Medicine, Aruba
	Doctor of Medicine
YR-8 to YR-5	Nita State University (night program)
	Bachelor of Science, Biology
YR-11 to YR-10	Nita State Police Academy
YR-15 to YR-11	Nita State University
	- Bachelor of Science, Criminal Justice
	- President of MADD chapter

PROFESSIONAL EXPERIENCE

YR-1 to present	Residency: Nita State Hospital
YR-11 to YR-5	Nita State Police
	- State Trooper
	- Certified DUI Testing Instructor

PROFESSIONAL ORGANIZATIONS

- Lifetime Member, Nita State Police Officers' Organization
- National Association Against Drunk Driving

PUBLICATIONS

"Blood Alcohol Content and Driver Impairment," *Nita Journal of Medicine*, YR-3. An in-depth examination of the relationship between BAC and driver impairment.

"Drunk Driving Enforcement Begins at Home," *MADD Annual Newsletter*, December YR-6. An article that serves as a practical guide to family intervention in the behaviors that lead to driving under the influence.

"Community Policing of Drunk Driving," *Nita Times Dispatch*, March 20, YR-10. An article suggesting that community groups, local governments, and educators have a critical role to play in the fight against drunk driving.

MEMORANDUM

TO: Counsel for Jordan Peyton
FROM: Fran Montgomery, MD, PhD
DATE: October 20, YR-1
RE: State v. Jordan Peyton

Per our agreement, I have reviewed the police report, Intoxilyzer test results, and Kipper Williams's analysis of the Peyton case. I have formulated an opinion as to the accuracy of Dr. Williams's conclusion that Peyton likely had a blood alcohol content (BAC) of between 0.09 and 0.11 and was operating her vehicle under the influence of alcohol at the time of the incident. I believe that Dr. Williams's analysis is faulty and that without consideration for Peyton's physiological attributes and other environmental factors, and without a BAC test taken closer to the time of driving, it is not possible to conclude within a reasonable degree of medical certainty that Peyton had a BAC higher than 0.06 or was impaired at the time she was driving.

Background and Agreement

You have agreed to compensate me at a rate of $200 per hour for my analysis and report drafting and $400 per hour for my in-court testimony. I have attached my CV for your reference. In addition to my traditional credentials, in YR-1 I was the recipient of the B. C. Woodward Foundation Grant for research in the area of the abuse of forensic evidence in legal proceedings. This is a $200,000 grant over the course of three years. I am researching decided legal cases that relied heavily on questionable scientific evidence. The goal of my research is to highlight the impact of science on legal proceedings and support stricter ethical rules governing the testimony of medical professionals at legal proceedings. All of my fees from this case will be invested in this research project.

In addition, I have never testified for the State on this or any other issue. If I am called to testify in this case, it will be the fifth time I have testified in court as an expert on this issue.

General Information

I have a particular interest in the use of BAC as evidence in DUI prosecutions. This is an area of concern to me because I believe courts rely too heavily on BAC as a determining factor in assessing impairment. There is no reliable science linking a particular individual's actual impairment with a generic BAC level. I have treated many intoxicated patients during my time in the emergency room, and I have witnessed individuals with the same BAC demonstrate vastly different degrees of impairment. Factors such as body weight, stomach contents, environmental contaminants such as gas fumes or cigarette smoke, and the presence of medications or fever in the body can all dramatically impact the BAC reading and the level of impairment between individuals with the same BAC.

Case-Specific Analysis

According to Peyton, she consumed two beers within a two-hour period on a relatively empty stomach. Peyton was also training for a marathon, which leads me to believe she may have a great deal of lean muscle mass and a low body fat percentage. Lean muscle contains more water, which absorbs alcohol from the bloodstream and works to lower BAC. A body with lean muscle mass can tolerate more alcohol than a body with little muscle mass, because a body with more lean muscle mass processes alcohol more slowly. This means, to use Dr. Williams's bell curve analysis, Peyton would move more slowly along the bell curve than an individual with less muscle mass. In addition, a person with more lean muscle mass may demonstrate less impairment than a person with high body fat content. This only scratches the surface of the physiological factors that should have been, but were not, considered by Dr. Williams.

The more troubling issue with the prosecution's reliance on Peyton's 0.06 BAC as evidence of any level of impairment when she was driving is that she was given the Intoxilyzer test at 9:30 p.m., nearly two hours after she was driving. This passage of time diminishes the reliability of the reading. In his analysis of Peyton's BAC, Dr. Williams assumes that her absorption of alcohol remained constant at all times throughout the alcohol metabolization process. This process does not occur at a uniform pace, with the body processing alcohol at the same rate over time. Rather, this process occurs at differing rates where during some periods more alcohol is processed, while during others, the rate slows down dramatically. Although this process generally resembles a bell curve, it is impossible to say with any high degree of medical probability what Peyton's BAC at an earlier time would have been. Any such opinion is merely a guess based on assumptions and conjecture, not science.

As you have asked me to give my opinion as to Peyton's likely BAC at the time she was driving, in my opinion, the alcohol level in Peyton's body was likely just peaking at the time of the Intoxilyzer test. Therefore, in my expert opinion, her BAC at the time she was driving would have been lower than the 0.06 that she registered when tested. This is consistent with my earlier statement that if Peyton's body had high lean muscle content, her body would process alcohol more slowly. It is also consistent with Peyton's claim that she only had two beers at the earlier event. I have attached my analysis, plotted on Dr. Williams's bell chart, to demonstrate how my position differs from Dr. Williams's position. If compelled to give a likely range of BAC when she was driving, I would estimate it to be between 0.03 and 0.05. Please keep in mind that I do not state this range to a reasonable degree of medical certainty, as that would be impossible after the passage of more than two hours from the time of driving and without a full report of Peyton's physiological attributes and other environment factors.

In my opinion, the Intoxilyzer results from Peyton's test are an unreliable indication of her BAC or her level of impairment during her driving. Dr. Williams's analysis is faulty because it does not take into consideration physiological and environmental factors and relies exclusively on the results of a BAC test performed two hours after the driving. Any extrapolation backward from the time of the test to determine Peyton's likely BAC or level of impairment at the time she was driving would be a mere guess. Further, to use a generic and fairly arbitrary BAC level such at 0.08 as a threshold to conclude that someone is impaired to the point of being unsafe fails to consider numerous factors that have been shown to impact impairment.

Bell Curve Chart According to Dr. Fran Montgomery

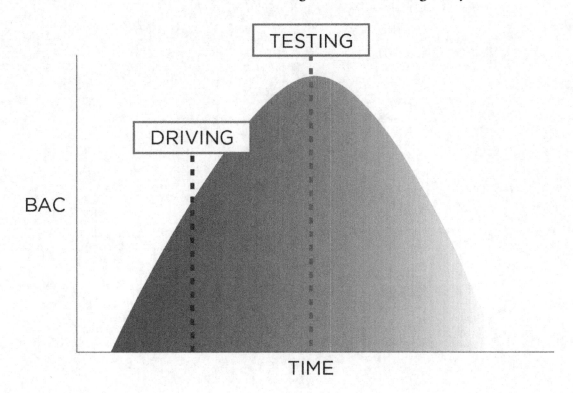

Fran Montgomery, MD, PhD

EDUCATION & PROFESSIONAL EXPERIENCE

YR-1—Present Attending Physician: Nita City Hospital
       Emergency Department

YR-3—YR-1   Columbia University
       PhD, Forensic Toxicology

YR-7—YR-3   Residency: Duke Hospital
       Internal Medicine

YR-11—YR-7   Duke University School of Medicine
       Doctor of Medicine
       Specialization in Toxicology and Internal Medicine
       Graduated *magna cum laude*

YR-15—YR-11   Duke University
       BS Biochemistry
       Graduated *magna cum laude*

PROFESSIONAL AFFILIATIONS & AWARDS

Recipient, B. C. Woodward Foundation Grant for research in the area of abuse of forensic evidence ($200,000 over three years, beginning YR-1)

Society of Forensic Toxicologists

American Academy of Forensic Sciences

The International Association of Forensic Toxicologists

PUBLICATIONS

"Drunks Rising: The Grey Science of Rising and Failing Curves of Drunkenness," *Legal Times*, December YR-1.
An article on the difficulty of determining blood alcohol content retroactively.

"Science on the Witness Stand," *Journal of Forensic Science*, May YR-2.
An article on the persuasive presentation of scientific information to jurors and lay people.

Exhibit 26

Affidavit to Certify Records

CUSTODIAN FOR NITA STATE UNIVERSITY HOSPITAL AND NITA PRIMARY PHYSCIANS GROUP

JAMES CONNERS, being duly sworn upon oath, deposes and states as follows:

1. My name is James Conners. I have personal knowledge of and can testify to each and every fact set forth in this Affidavit.

2. I have been the records custodian for Nita State University Hospital since YR-11.

3. I have been the records custodian for Nita Primary Physicians Group since YR-10.

4. I have reviewed the following medical records and can certify them to being authentic and that each of these records is a public record:

    a. Nita State University Hospital Discharge Summary Form

    b. Nita Primary Physicians Group Medical Visit

    c. Second Nita Primary Physicians Group Medical Visit

DATED this 20th day of January, YR-0.

James Conners

Records Custodian

      SUBSCRIBED AND SWORN to before me this 20th day of January, YR-0.

Tyler Farkle
Tyler Farkle
Public Notary
My commission expires: 07/27/YR+4

Exhibit 27

Hospital Discharge Summary Form

Patient Name	Taylor Addison		DOB: 04/15/YR-35	
Address	447 Lockney Drive, Jamesburg Columbia 85467	Phone#	Home:	Office:
PCP Name	Nita Primary Physicians Group		Medical group: Primary	Insurance: Blue Group Insurance Policy # WF3030X
Facility Name	NITA STATE UNIVERSITY HOSPITAL		Attending physician	Dr. Pat Nelson, MD

1. You were admitted to NITA STATE UNIVERSITY HOSPITAL on the following date 05/15/YR-1
Admitted to Emergency Department on 05/15/YR-1.
2. At admission you presented with the following symptoms:
Burns to left hand caused by spilled coffee during car accident.
3. You were diagnosed with
First- and second-degree burns to left hand.
4. You were evaluated by
Dr. Nelson, MD.
5. You are now (list current treatment plan and/or state the medical issue is resolved)
Discharged with instruction to follow up with primary care in 2 weeks to assess for possible infection and status of healing.
6. Your provider feels that your condition has improved and that the care you need now could safely be provided in/at
Nita Primary Physicians Group
7. Your discharge plan and follow-up care include
Take pain medication every four (4) hours as needed for pain management. Apply clean gauze and bandages to the wound every six (6) hours. Reassess pain level at follow-up visit with primary care physician. See doctor immediately if you experience any abnormal side effects.

Print Name of the person completing the form	Dr. Pat Nelson, MD	
Signature of the person completing the form	*Pat Nelson*	Phone # 819-555-2413
Patient Name Printed	Taylor Addison	
Patient Signature	Taylor Addison	Date 05/15/YR-1	

Exhibit 28

Nita Primary Physicians Group Medical Visit

Nita Primary Physicians Group

Patient Name: Taylor Addison

DOB: 04/15/YR-35

Visit Information:

05/29/YR-1

Reasons for visit: Received burn on 05/15/YR-1. Initially treated at ER. Diagnosed with first- and second-degree burns.

Michelle Randall, MD

Nita Primary Physicians Group

(748)-487-3751

11715 Crossway Blvd

Nita City, Nita

Assessments

- No signs of infection

- Burn healing well

Care Plan

- Change dressings and apply antibiotic ointment 2x/day for one week

- After one week, apply dressings only at night

- Call if increasing redness, swelling, sign of infection

- Follow up in six weeks

Physician Signature: *MR*   Date: 05/29/YR-1

Exhibit 29

Second Nita Primary Physicians Group Medical Visit

Nita Primary Physicians Group

Patient Name: Taylor Addison

DOB: 04/15/YR-35

Visit Information:

07/10/YR-1

Reasons for visit: Follow-up after burn received 05/15/YR-1. Initially treated at ER. Diagnosed with first- and second-degree burns. First visit to NPPG for this condition was on 05/29/YR-1. Michelle Randall, MD

Nita Primary Physicians Group
(748)-487-3751
11715 Crossway Blvd
Nita City, Nita

Assessments

- Burn completely healed

- Slight signs of scarring (potentially permanent)

- Patient reported sensitivity in left hand

Care Plan

- Return to primary care as needed. No further follow-up visits required.

Physician Signature: *MR*   Date: 07/10/YR-1

APPENDICES

NITA STATUTES

Nita Criminal Code—Article 4

Section 4-101 Duty of Driver to Stop, Etc., in Event of Accident Involving Injury or Death or Damage to Attended Property

The driver of any motor vehicle who is knowingly involved in an accident in which a person is killed or injured, or in which an occupied vehicle is damaged, shall immediately stop as close to the scene of the accident as possible without obstructing traffic and report his or her: (a) name, (b) address, (c) driver's license number, and (d) vehicle registration to the local law-enforcement agency, and to: (a) the person struck or injured if that person seems capable of understanding and retaining the information, (b) if present, some other occupant of the vehicle collided with, or (c) the custodian of the injured property.

The driver shall also render reasonable assistance to any person injured in such accident. "Accident," for purposes of this Article, is defined as any unintentional or intentional contact between a motor vehicle and another motor vehicle, train, person, animal, or inanimate object that results in damage or injury, no matter how slight.

Violation of this section is a felony punishable for up to ten years in prison and/or a $2,500 fine.

Nita Criminal Code—Article 6

Section 6-101 Driving Motor Vehicle under the Influence of Intoxicants

It shall be unlawful for any person to operate any motor vehicle on a public roadway while such person is under the influence of alcohol or any other self-administered intoxicant or drug of any nature, or any combination of such drugs to a degree that impairs his or her ability to drive or operate any motor vehicle safely.

Section 6-201 Implied Consent to Post-Arrest Testing to Determine Drug or Alcohol Content of Blood

Any person, whether licensed by the State of Nita or not, who operates a motor vehicle in the State of Nita shall be deemed thereby, as a condition of such operation, to have consented to have samples of his or her blood, breath, or both blood and breath taken for a chemical test to determine the alcohol and/or drug content of his or her blood, if he or she is arrested for violation of driving a motor vehicle while intoxicated, within two hours of the alleged offense.

Section 6-202 Presumptions from Alcohol Content of Blood

In any prosecution for a violation of § 6-101, the amount of alcohol in the blood of the accused at the time of the alleged offense, as indicated by a chemical analysis of a sample of the accused's blood or breath to determine the alcohol content of his or her blood, shall give rise to the following rebuttable presumptions:

A. If there was at that time 0.08 percent or more by weight by volume of alcohol in the accused's blood or 0.08 grams or more per 210 liters of the accused's breath, it shall be presumed that the accused was under the influence of alcoholic intoxicants.

B. If there was at that time less than 0.08 percent by weight by volume of alcohol in the accused's blood or less than 0.08 grams per 210 liters of the accused's breath, such fact shall not give rise to any presumption that the accused was or was not under the influence of alcoholic intoxicants, but such fact may be considered with other competent evidence in determining the guilt or innocence of the accused.

Nita Criminal Code—Article 10

Section 10-101 Admissibility of Certified Court and Agency Records

The records of any judicial proceeding and any other official records of a court or State agency, if otherwise admissible, shall be received into evidence without the testimony of the record's custodian, provided that such records are authenticated and certified by the clerk of the court or agency having legal custody of the record.

Section 10-107 Admissibility of Blood Alcohol Content Test Results

Blood Alcohol Content (BAC) test results shall be admissible in a criminal or civil matter as long as the following requirements are satisfied:

A. the test was conducted by a certified administrator for the specific equipment used to test the sample;

B. the administrator's certification was made by a state agency, and a document of certification is available for the court's review; and

C. the equipment was in proper working order at the time of the test.

CASE LAW

State v. Jacobs, 10 Nita 325 (YR-15). A defendant who was seated in a car with the engine off without wearing a seat belt is not guilty of the crime of failing to wear a seat belt. The plain language of the statute suggests that the legislature only intended that seat belts be worn when the car is either "moving or the engine is engaged."

State v. Michaels, 15 Nita 100 (YR-10). This case reaffirmed the specific intent of "knowingly" for the crime of hit and run under Nita Criminal Code Section 4-101. The plain language of the statute suggests that the legislature intended for a defendant to be guilty of this crime only when the defendant "knowingly hit a vehicle and fled the scene." In *Michaels*, the court held that the defendant was not guilty because there was no evidence the defendant knew or should have known that he hit the victim's car.

State v. Daniels, 23 Nita 120 (YR-5). The criminal case law in Nita mandates that in order for a breath test to be admissible using an Intoxilyzer, the test must be given within two hours of the defendant driving the vehicle. In *Daniels*, the defendant was given the test two hours and twenty minutes after driving, and the court held the test results were inadmissible because they were an unreliable indicator of the BAC of the defendant when driving.

Related Material

Information on Burns

Thermal Burns

Thermal burns are caused by any hot or heated source such as a flame, scald (from steam, hot or molten liquid), or contact (from a hot object, such as a hot cooking pan). While most thermal burns are mild, some may be quite severe. The severity of the burn depends on the number of layers of skin affected. The severity of burns can be either referred to by degrees (first, second, third) or their thickness (superficial, partial, and full).

Types of Burns

First-Degree Burn or Superficial Burn

This burn only affects the epidermis, or the outer layer of the skin. The symptoms of this kind of burn are a painful, red area that turns white when touched. There are not usually blisters.

Second-Degree Burn or Partial-Thickness Burn

This burn affects the epidermis and some portions of the dermis, the second layer of the skin. Depending on how much of the dermis is involved, this can be further characterized as superficial or deep.

A superficial partial-thickness burn is painful and red, turning white when touched. There are often blisters and mottling. Hairs are still present.

A deep partial-thickness burn may or may not be painful depending on whether the burn is deep enough to burn the nerve endings. Hair is usually gone from the area of the burn.

Skin Burns

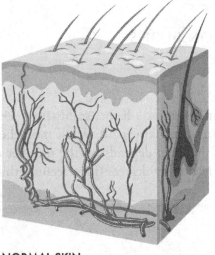

NORMAL SKIN

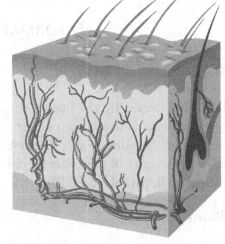

FIRST DEGREE BURN

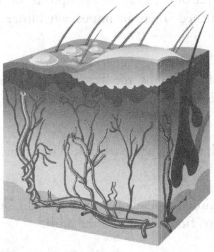

SECOND DEGREE BURN

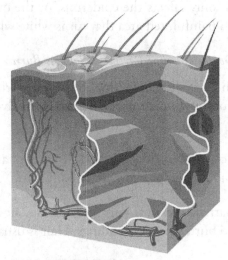

THIRD DEGREE BURN

Third-Degree Burn or Full-Thickness Burn

This burn is the most severe kind of burn. It burns all of the epidermis and dermis, and nerve endings, blood vessels, hair follicles, and sweat glands are all destroyed. If the burn is very severe, it may involve bone and muscle. This kind of burn is painless, with no sensation to touch. The appearance is usually pearly white or charred and may appear leathery.

INFORMATION ON BREATH TESTS AND INTOXILYZER

Why a Breath Test?

Breath testing for alcohol is based upon the principle that alcohol is excreted unchanged in human breath because of equilibrium conditions between lung capillaries and pulmonary alveoli. At constant temperatures, the amount of alcohol in the breath is proportional to the amount of alcohol in the blood.

Method

The process begins when a person breathes into the machine. A quartz lamp then radiates infrared energy, which travels through a chamber that contains the person's breath. After leaving the chamber, a lens focuses the energy into a chopper wheel containing three narrowband infrared filters. The infrared energy passed by the filters is focused on a highly sensitive photodetector that converts the infrared pulses into electrical pulses. The microprocessor interprets the pulses and calculates the BAC that is then displayed.

The Intoxilyzer

The Intoxilyzer, in particular, uses infrared spectrometry to measure alcohol concentration in a breath sample. The instrument measures the degree alcohol absorbs infrared energy; the more alcohol present, the greater the absorption.

Operating the Intoxilyzer is simple. A single push of a button controls the entire breath sequence. Further, there is a digital display along with audible tones that guides the operator through the test, preventing any procedural errors. Once the test is complete, test results are printed on a three-part carbonless evidence card.

Proposed Jury Instructions

These instructions are taken from the Nita Model Jury Instructions and reflect the current law of Nita.

1) You have been selected and sworn in as jurors. You must arrive at your verdict by unanimous vote. You must base your verdict on the facts and the law. First, you must determine the facts from the evidence presented in the trial and not from any other source. Second, you must accept and follow the law as I state it to you, regardless of whether you agree with it.

2) The State of Nita has charged the defendant with the crimes of driving under the influence of intoxicants, and felonious hit and run. The defendant has pleaded not guilty.

3) To prove the crime of driving under the influence of intoxicants, the state must prove all the following propositions:

   a) while operating a motor vehicle;

   b) on a public roadway;

   c) the defendant was under the influence of alcohol, or any other self-administered intoxicant or drug of any nature, or any combination of such drugs, to a degree as to impair his/her ability to drive or operate a motor vehicle safely.

If you find from your consideration of all the evidence that each of these propositions has been proved beyond a reasonable doubt, then you should find the defendant guilty of driving under the influence of intoxicants.

If, on the other hand, you find from your consideration of all the evidence that any of these propositions has not been proven beyond a reasonable doubt, then you should find the defendant not guilty of driving under the influence of intoxicants.

4) To prove the crime of felonious hit and run, the state must prove all the following propositions:

   a) while operating a motor vehicle, the defendant knew that he or she was involved in an accident;

   b) as a result of the accident, a person was injured or an occupied vehicle was damaged; and

   c) the defendant failed to stop as close to the scene of the accident as possible without obstructing traffic and report his or her (1) name, (2) address, (3) driver's license number, and (4) vehicle registration to the local law-enforcement agency, and to (1) the person struck or injured if that person seems capable of understanding and retaining the information, (2) if present, some other occupant of the vehicle collided with, or (3) to the custodian of the injured property.

"Accident" for purposes of this case means any unintentional or intentional contact between a motor vehicle and another motor vehicle that results in damage, no matter how slight.

If you find from your consideration of all the evidence that each of these propositions has been proven beyond a reasonable doubt, then you should find the defendant guilty of felonious hit and run.

If, on the other hand, you find from your consideration of all the evidence that any of these propositions has not been proved beyond a reasonable doubt, then you should find the defendant not guilty of felonious hit and run.

Blood Alcohol Content as Evidence of Impairment.

You may consider the amount of alcohol in the defendant's blood at the time of the alleged offense as indicated by a chemical analysis of a sample of the defendant's blood or breath.

If you find that there was, at the time of the offense, 0.08 grams of alcohol or more per 210 liters of the defendant's breath, you shall presume that the defendant was under the influence of alcoholic intoxicants. The defendant may rebut this presumption.

If, however, you find that there was, at the time of the offense, less than 0.08 grams of alcohol per 210 liters of the defendant's breath, such fact shall not give rise to any presumption that the defendant was or was not under the influence of alcoholic intoxicants, but such fact may be considered with other competent evidence in determining the guilt or innocence of the defendant.

Direct and Circumstantial Evidence.

The law recognizes two kinds of evidence—direct and circumstantial. Direct evidence proves a fact directly without further need for other evidence. Circumstantial evidence is a fact or circumstance that, if proven, provides a basis for a reasonable inference of another fact or facts.

The law makes no distinction between direct and circumstantial evidence as to the degree or amount of proof required, and each should be considered according to whatever weight or value it may have. All of the evidence, direct and circumstantial, should be considered and evaluated by you in arriving at your verdict.

[Optional Instruction]

Expert Testimony.

You heard testimony in this case from witnesses with special knowledge, skill, experience, training, or education in a particular subject. These types of witnesses are referred to as expert witnesses. In determining what weight to give to the testimony of the expert witnesses, you should consider the qualifications and believability of the witness, the facts upon which each opinion is based, and the reasons for each opinion. You are not bound by the opinion of any expert witness. Give each opinion the weight you find it deserves. You may disregard any opinion if you find it to be unreasonable.

**IN THE CIRCUIT COURT
FOR THE CITY OF NITA**

THE PEOPLE OF THE STATE OF NITA   )
)
         v.   )   Case No. CR 1112
)

JORDAN PEYTON   )
)

Defendant.   )

VERDICT

We, the jury, return the following verdict, and each of us concurs in this verdict: [Choose the appropriate verdict]

FELONIOUS HIT AND RUN

On the charge of felonious hit and run, we, the jury, find the defendant, Jordan Peyton:

_____ GUILTY
_____ NOT GUILTY

                                         _____
                                         Presiding Juror

DRIVING UNDER THE INFLUENCE OF INTOXICANTS

On the charge of driving under the influence of intoxicants, we, the jury, find the defendant, Jordan Peyton:

_____ GUILTY
_____ NOT GUILTY

                                         _____
                                         Presiding Juror